EXCAVATING THE PAST

ANCIENT EGYPT

Jackie Gaff

Heinemann
LIBRARY

www.heinemann.co.uk/library

Visit our website to find out more information about Heinemann Library books.

To order:
- ☎ Phone 44 (0) 1865 888066
- 🖷 Send a fax to 44 (0) 1865 314091
- 💻 Visit the Heinemann Bookshop at www.heinemann.co.uk/library to browse our catalogue and order online.

First published in Great Britain by
Heinemann Library, Halley Court,
Jordan Hill, Oxford OX2 8EJ,
part of Harcourt Education.

Heinemann is a registered trademark of
Harcourt Education Ltd.

© Harcourt Education Ltd 2004
First published in paperback in 2005
The moral right of the proprietor has
been asserted.

Editorial: Nicole Irving, Kate Bellamy and
Ruth Nason
Design: Carole Binding
Picture Research: Shelley Noronha
Production: Edward Moore

Originated by Ambassador Litho Ltd
Printed in China by WKT

ISBN 0 431 14237 8 (hardback)
08 07 06 05 04
10 9 8 7 6 5 4 3 2 1

ISBN 0 431 14244 0 (paperback)
09 08 07 06 05
10 9 8 7 6 5 4 3 2 1

British Library Cataloguing in Publication Data

Jackie Gaff
Ancient Egypt. – (Excavating the Past)
932
A full catalogue record for this book is
available from the British Library.

Acknowledgements

The publishers would like to thank the
following for permission to reproduce
photographs: Art Archive: pp. **6**, **8**, **9** top, **9**
bottom, **10**, **11** top, **12**, **14** top, **14** bottom, **16**,
18 top, **19** bottom, **24**, **25** top, **25** bottom, **26**,
27, **28** left, **28** right, **29** top, **29** bottom, **30**, **32**,
33 top, **33** right, **34** top, **34** bottom, **35** top, **35**
bottom, **36**, **38** left, **39**, **40**, **41** top, **41** bottom;
Bridgeman Art Library: pp. **5**, **15** bottom, **21**
top, **21** bottom, **22**, **23**, **33** bottom; Corbis:
7(Hulton-Deutsch Collection); Science Photo
Library: pp. **15** top (Alexander Tsiaras),
43 (Philippe Plailly, Eurelios); Werner Forman:
pp. **13**, **19** top, **38** right.

Cover photograph of the Great Sphinx and
the Great Pyramid at Giza reproduced with
permission of Digital Stock. The small
photograph of the death mask that covered
Tutankhamen's mummy reproduced with
permission of Werner Forman Archive.

The Publishers would like to thank
Richard Parkinson, at the British Museum,
for his assistance with the preparation of
this book.

CONTENTS

Dates BC and AD

BC after a date means before the birth of Christ. The years count down to 0, the date that has been taken as the year when Jesus Christ was born.

AD before a date stands for the Latin *anno domini* ('the year of the lord'). It means that the date is counted from after Christ's birth in the year 0.

The Ancient Egyptian World 4
    The development of archaeology 6

Unlocking the Language 8
    The Rosetta Stone...9
    Egyptian scribes and scholars 10

Mummies and the Afterlife 12
    The royal tomb at Deir el-Bahri 12
    Making a mummy 14

The Pyramid Builders 16
    The Great Pyramid at Giza 16
    Pyramid designers and builders 18

Pharaohs and Government 20
    The Valley of the Kings 20
    Tutankhamen's treasures 22
    Finding out about the pharaoh...................................24

Temples and Gods 26
    The great temple complex at Karnak 26
    Priests and worshippers..28

Everyday Life of the Wealthy 30
    The tomb of Nebamun..30
    Pastimes 32
    Fashion...34

Everyday Life of the Workers 36
    The workers' village of Deir el-Medina.....................36
    People at work 38
    Farming and food..40

Archaeology Today 42

Timeline of Ancient Egypt.. 44
Timeline of Egyptology 45
Glossary 46
Index..48

Any words appearing in the text in bold, **like this**, are explained in the Glossary.

THE ANCIENT EGYPTIAN WORLD

Nearly 5000 years have passed since the ancient Egyptians began creating one of the world's earliest, greatest and longest-lasting civilizations. In their lands beside the River Nile, they founded magnificent cities where all kinds of knowledge flourished, from **astronomy** and **engineering** to mathematics and medicine. The Egyptians' most awe-inspiring achievements were in art and architecture. They carved amazing sculptures and decorated walls with fabulous paintings. They built vast **temples**, and gigantic stone pyramids as **tombs** for their rulers, the **pharaohs**.

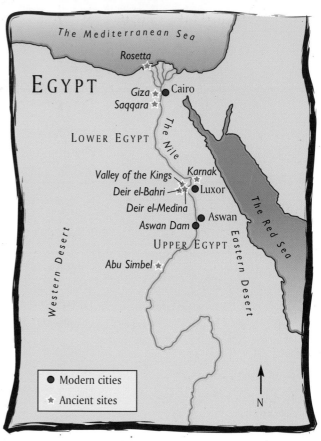

Out with the old

The civilization flourished for nearly 3000 years, but eventually Egypt was weakened by **civil war** and invasion by foreign powers. In 332 BC, Egypt was invaded by the Greeks, led by Alexander the Great, and became part of his empire. Nearly 300 years later it was conquered by the Romans. In the following centuries the Christian religion was introduced to Egypt, and churches and monasteries replaced the ancient temples as centres of worship. In the 7th century AD, Egypt was invaded by Arab peoples and became the mainly Muslim country it is today.

△ The Egyptian civilization would not have developed without the River Nile. The fertile land beside it could be farmed, whereas the regions to the west and east were barren desert. The Nile provided fish and other animals to eat, and mud for making pots and building houses. It was also Egypt's main highway, with people travelling the length of the country by boat.

EYEWITNESS

'I was treading the soil of a land covered since immemorial times [times beyond memory] with a veil of mystery.'

(Domenique Vivant Denon, leader of the artists who accompanied Napoleon's army to Egypt in 1798)

Lost in the mists of time

The ancient Egyptian language and way of life were slowly lost. Many buildings were destroyed or buried beneath rubble and sand, but larger stone structures, such as the great temples and pyramids, survived. Egypt became popular with foreign sightseers from Greek and Roman times onwards, but although travellers wondered at the ancient stone monuments, no one knew what they were. **Medieval** European **pilgrims**, for instance, remembered the Bible story about Joseph storing up grain during Egypt's seven years of **famine** and thought that the pyramids were his granaries.

In with the new

Proper scientific study of the ancient remains only began in 1798, when the French emperor Napoleon and his army invaded Egypt. The French were defeated by the British and forced to leave Egypt in 1801. However, a team of artists and scientists had travelled with Napoleon's army, to record all they could discover about Egypt, ancient and modern. The team carried out the first detailed **survey** of ancient Egyptian monuments and laid the foundations of **Egyptology** – the study of the language, culture and history of ancient Egypt.

▽ *This engraving from a book by Domenique Vivant Denon about Napoleon's expedition to Egypt in 1798, shows French scientists measuring the Great Sphinx at Giza.*

DID YOU KNOW? Ancient Greek and Roman tourists carved graffiti on ancient Egyptian monuments.

5

The development of archaeology

Hunting for treasure

The findings of Napoleon's artists started a worldwide fashion for collecting ancient **artefacts** or objects (called **antiquities** at that time), and collectors flocked to Egypt in the early 19th century. Unfortunately, most were interested only in discovering unusual or valuable antiquities such as gold jewellery, and they did not care how much damage they did in the process. Battering rams and even explosives were used to open up sites, and so countless everyday objects were lost forever, along with a wealth of information. Other sites were robbed by local people, for antiquities they could sell to foreigners.

◁ *Many antiquities were taken out of Egypt in the early 19th century, and some of them formed the basis of the great collections now held in museums around the world. This painting shows a statue of the pharaoh Rameses II being taken from Luxor for a dealer called Giovanni Belzoni. The statue is now in the British Museum, London.*

Rescue operation

The situation was saved largely by Frenchman Auguste Mariette (1821–81), who arrived in Egypt in 1850. Mariette was determined to stop the looting and destruction of antiquities, and to make sure that finds were properly studied and cared for. In 1858, the Egyptian ruler Said Pasha made him director of the new Egyptian Antiquities Service. It was Mariette's responsibility to supervise all **excavations** in Egypt and to police the **export** of antiquities. He was also given permission to set up Egypt's first museum of antiquities, the Egyptian Museum in Cairo.

WHO WAS Sir William Flinders Petrie?

*Sir William Flinders Petrie was one of the first scientific excavators in the history of Egyptian archaeology, establishing techniques that are still used today. He was born in England in 1853 and travelled to Egypt in the early 1880s. By the time he left in 1923, he had led excavations at almost every major site in the country. He continued working on **digs** until shortly before he died, at the grand age of 89, in 1942.*

Pioneering practice

The late 19th century saw the development of true **archaeology** – the scientific excavation and study of the remains of past civilizations. In Egypt, its pioneers included Englishman Sir William Flinders Petrie (1853–1942) and American George Reisner (1867–1942). Both men understood the value of careful excavation, and of recording everything they found. They knew that everything discovered, from pottery and bones to artwork and buildings, can provide clues about how people once lived and died. It is thanks to the practice of scientific archaeology that so much evidence has survived to tell us the story of everyday life in ancient Egyptian times.

Archaeology Challenge

Petrie invented a way of dating and classifying objects by their appearance, which is known as sequence dating. Through studying **prehistoric** pots, he realized that their shapes and patterns differed over time and could give useful clues about when they were made. Although modern techniques for dating objects, such as **radiocarbon dating**, are more exact, sequence dating is still used to give a rough date to objects found on digs.

UNLOCKING THE LANGUAGE

Written evidence is enormously important in helping **archaeologists** to find out about the past. The ancient Egyptians were among the first people to use writing, and a range of written records, from legal documents to letters and poems, have helped us to piece their story together. But, at first, archaeologists had a problem: no one knew how to read Egyptian writing.

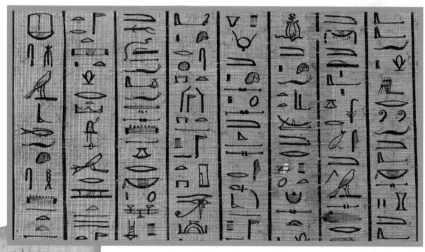

▽ *This example of ancient Egyptian writing on papyrus dates from the 1st century BC.*

Archaeology Challenge

Epigraphy is a branch of archaeology concerned with recording **inscriptions**, such as writings, carvings and paintings. The first official epigraphers began work in Egypt in the 1890s and, although equipment has improved over the years, the techniques have remained much the same. A photograph is taken. Then the photographed inscription is traced in ink. Finally, the tracing is compared with the original to check that the record is accurate.

Lost languages

Instead of an alphabet, the Egyptians wrote with picture symbols, called **hieroglyphs**. Most of the symbols stood for sounds, but some stood for ideas. Two other scripts evolved from hieroglyphs, called **hieratic** and **demotic**. In about the 1st century BC, the **Coptic** script developed – this was written with the 24 letters of the Greek alphabet and six signs taken from demotic. Coptic slowly replaced the other three scripts and within a few hundred years there was no one left who could understand them.

The Rosetta Stone

The key to translating ancient Egyptian writing was found at Rosetta in 1799, by a soldier in Napoleon's army. The Rosetta Stone is a large slab of polished granite, dating from the 2nd century BC. It has the same text carved into it in three languages – hieroglyphic, demotic and Greek, the language spoken by Egypt's ruling classes after the country was absorbed into the Greek Empire. It is thought to have been carved in 196 BC. Copies were made of the carvings and studied by scholars who understood ancient Greek. Some of them realized that the royal names they could read in the Greek text were the words in **cartouches** in the hieroglyphic text. Others used their knowledge of Coptic to work out what some of the demotic signs stood for. Finally, in 1822, Jean-François Champollion cracked the code of the Rosetta Stone, becoming the first person since ancient times to understand the meaning of Egyptian hieroglyphs.

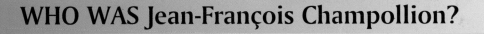

WHO WAS Jean-François Champollion?

Born in France in 1790, Champollion became passionate about languages at school, studying Latin, Greek, Arabic, Coptic and other ancient languages. He published his first book on Egypt when he was 21 and solved the mystery of the hieroglyphs in 1822, when he was 32. He visited Egypt only once, in 1828–29. He died after a stroke in 1832.

▷ *After the British defeated Napoleon's army in 1801, the Rosetta Stone was taken to the British Museum in London, where it still is today.*

Egyptian scribes and scholars

Most of the written evidence we have from ancient Egyptian times was created by educated men called **scribes**. All the top jobs in the government, army and priesthood were held by scribes. Most other scribes worked as ordinary civil servants, doing everything from collecting taxes to recording law cases. Others became scholars or artists, or worked as teachers or librarians.

Being a good scribe was a passport to success, but only wealthy families could afford to educate their children. Ordinary children did not go to school. Instead, their fathers taught them a trade. Education was also only for boys. A few girls may have learned to read and write, but most stayed at home and were taught household skills by their mothers.

EYEWITNESS

'Be a scribe! It saves you from labour and protects you from all kinds of work. It spares you from using the hoe and the mattock ... It saves you from having to row a boat ...'

(Ancient Egyptian advice to a schoolboy)

Sitting like a scribe

In Egyptian art, scribes are usually shown sitting cross-legged, with a **papyrus scroll** on their lap. The scroll is in their left hand, leaving the right hand free for writing – although there must have been left-handed scribes, too! In reality also, scribes would sometimes stand to work or squat at a low desk. Schoolboys would sit cross-legged for lessons.

Gaining a good education

Boys who did go to school started at about five years old. They learned hieratic script at first, and practised by copying out sayings and stories on wooden boards or on pieces of broken pot and stone chips, called **ostraca**. Teachers were strict, and badly behaved students were beaten. As boys grew older and got the hang of hieratic, they began studying hieroglyphs. Older boys were also taught mathematics, while some studied **astronomy**, geography, history or law. By their teens, they were ready to leave school and start work.

Perfect papyrus

Papyrus paper was one of the Egyptians' most useful inventions, made from the tall papyrus reeds that grew on the banks of the River Nile. The reeds were peeled and soaked, then sliced into strips, which were beaten flat and laid on top of one another in a criss-cross pattern to form a square sheet. Next the sheet was pressed under a heavy weight, while the strips dried and stuck together. The final stage was to glue several sheets together with gum, to make a scroll.

Writing cases

This hieroglyphic sign shows a scribe's basic writing equipment. The upside-down U represents a strap, which went over the scribe's shoulder. From it hangs a wooden palette, with two round holes for holding solid cakes of black and red ink. At the other end of the strap are a pot for the water the scribe used to wet his inks and a container for his reed pens. The hieroglyph represents the sound 'sesh', and when followed by the sign for a man, it meant 'scribe'.

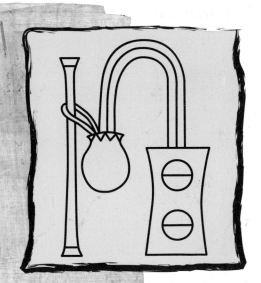

MUMMIES AND THE AFTERLIFE

Archaeologists collect clues about the past from the bodies and possessions people left behind, as well as from written evidence. And the ancient Egyptians left a wealth of **artefacts** behind them, including hundreds of preserved bodies called **mummies**. Mummification is a process in which a dead body is dried out to stop it from rotting. The Egyptians practised it because they believed in a life after death in which people still needed their bodies and possessions.

Mummifying a body properly was a long and costly process, so it was mainly practised by the wealthy. Then the mummies were placed in **tombs**, with all the objects they would need in the **Afterlife**. The most splendid burials were given to the rulers of Egypt, the **pharaohs**.

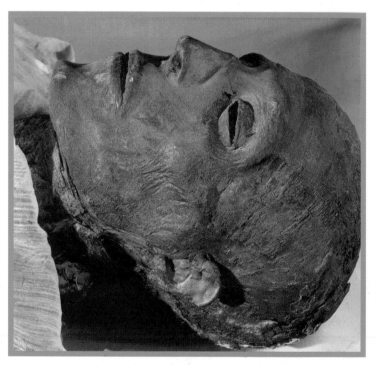

▽ *One of the mummies found at Deir el-Bahri was that of the pharaoh Seti I (reigned 1294–1279 BC). It is one of the best preserved of all the pharaohs' mummies that have been discovered so far.*

The royal tomb at Deir el-Bahri

It was not until the 1870s that any royal mummies were discovered. Then a family of Egyptian tomb-robbers stumbled across a hidden rock shaft at Deir el-Bahri, near the Valley of the Kings. Inside was a narrow corridor littered with piles of dusty wooden **coffins** and hundreds of precious **burial goods**, including **papyri** and funeral figurines.

For ten years the tomb-robbers kept their discovery secret, stealing the burial goods and selling them to dealers. But so many precious things appeared on the market that the Egyptian Antiquities Service decided to investigate where they were coming from. The tomb-robbers were tracked down, arrested and forced to lead the German Egyptologist Emile Brugsch (1842–1930) to their hoard. To his amazement, when he read the names on the coffins, Brugsch realized that they contained many of the greatest rulers in Egyptian history. More than 50 pharaohs, queens, other royals and **courtiers** were buried there. This was one of the most important finds in the history of **Egyptology**.

Archaeology Challenge

Although **archaeological** treasures are still sometimes found by accident, archaeologists today have a range of sophisticated equipment to help them hunt below ground. Radar is short for RAdio Direction And Ranging. It detects the position of objects by sending out radio signals towards them and interpreting the way the signals are bounced back. Developed in the 1930s, radar was not used on archaeological sites until the early 1990s. It has proved particularly useful in finding underground hollows, such as tunnels and tombs.

EYEWITNESS

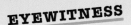

'I made the best examination of them [the coffins] I could by the light of my torch, and at once saw that they contained the mummies of royal personages of both sexes.'

(Emile Brugsch, describing his discovery at Deir el-Bahri on 6 July 1881)

Making a mummy

No ancient Egyptian description of the mummification process has been found, but we do have an eyewitness account from the Greek traveller and historian Herodotus (c. 485–425 BC), who visited Egypt in about 450 BC. Modern scientific analysis of mummies has proved that his description was fairly accurate.

The process took 70 days and began with washing and cleansing the body. The brain was hooked out through the nose and thrown away. Then a slit was cut in the left side of the body and the intestines, liver, lungs and stomach were removed. These four organs were preserved separately and later placed in special **canopic jars**. The heart was left in the body.

The next stage involved covering the body in a natural salt, called natron, which dried the body out and killed the bacteria that cause decay. After about 40 days, the natron was washed off and the body was stuffed with linen or sawdust. The skin was massaged with ointments to make it supple, and the body was coated in resin to make it waterproof.

△ *Mummification was carried out by special priests, who sometimes wore head masks to show that they represented the jackal-headed god Anubis, guardian of the dead.*

Canopic jars

Canopic jars held the dead person's mummified organs. The jars were often sealed with stoppers shaped like the heads of the four sons of Horus, one of the chief Egyptian gods. The Egyptians believed that this would place the organs under the gods' protection. Ape-headed Hapy (left) looked after the lungs. Hawk-headed Qebehsenuef looked after the intestines. Dog-headed Duamutef protected the stomach, and human-headed Imsety the liver.

Archaeology Challenge

In the past, mummies were often damaged when they were unwrapped by people keen to discover how they were preserved. Modern scientific techniques allow archaeologists to study mummies without damaging them. Sometimes a computerized piece of hospital equipment, called a CAT scanner, is used. This takes a series of X-rays of the body, then puts them together to produce a 3-D image which can be viewed from all angles.

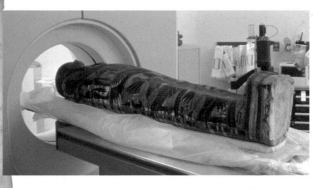

△ *A mummy inside its painted wooden coffin is about to enter a CAT scanning machine.*

The body was then wrapped from head to foot with linen bandages. The last layer was a shroud – a large piece of linen wrapped around the entire body. The mummy's face was covered with a mask that showed a portrait of the dead person. Finally, the mummy was laid inside a coffin, or sometimes a series of coffins, one inside the other. It was now ready for the funeral.

Cosy coffin

Coffins were often made of wood, which was then plastered and decorated. The face on the lid was an idealized portrait of the dead person.
This coffin belonged to a priestess who died about 3000 years ago. The lower half is decorated with paintings of gods and prayers to protect the priestess on the journey to the Afterlife.
When nobles and royalty were buried, their wooden coffins were placed inside a large stone one, called a **sarcophagus**.

THE PYRAMID BUILDERS

The **mummies** of Egyptian **pharaohs** were placed in special **tombs** designed to keep them safe throughout the **Afterlife**. The largest and most famous of these tombs are the pyramids, but unfortunately they were not as safe as their builders hoped. Tomb-robbing was practised from ancient times onwards. Archaeologists have now excavated more than 100 pyramids, but found that all of them had been broken into by tomb-robbers. None of them contained any of the pharaohs' mummies.

The Great Pyramid at Giza

Even so, the pyramids were a magnificent feat of **engineering**. They were built thousands of years ago, and yet many of them still stand today, towering above the desert sand. The largest is the Great Pyramid at Giza, to the west of the modern-day Egyptian capital, Cairo.

▽ *This is what the Great Pyramid at Giza looks like today, more than 4500 years after it was built. When new, the whole structure was topped with a triangular capstone and encased in huge slabs of polished white limestone which gleamed and glistened in the sunlight.*

▷ Inside the Great Pyramid are three chambers, linked by corridors. The pharaoh's empty sarcophagus was found in the King's chamber and remains there today. The two other burial chambers were never completed or used.

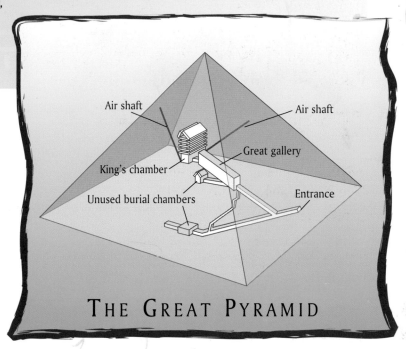

Air shaft   Air shaft
Great gallery
King's chamber
Unused burial chambers   Entrance

THE GREAT PYRAMID

This pyramid was the tomb of the pharaoh Khufu (reigned 2569–2566 BC). It was 146.6 metres (481 feet) high when finished. Work began in the mid-2500s BC and took 20 years. A staggering 2.5 million blocks of limestone went into the pyramid, each weighing around 2.5 tonnes!

Centuries of secrets

Egyptologists have been attempting to uncover the secrets of the pyramids ever since the first detailed **surveys** by experts travelling with Napoleon's army. Archaeologists have explored and mapped the pyramids inside and out, yet the discoveries continue. In 1993, for instance, archaeologists sent a robot camera into a narrow shaft leading upwards from one of the two unused burial chambers in the Great Pyramid. To their amazement, the robot photographed a stone door with two copper handles. For nine years people wondered what lay behind the door – hidden treasures, perhaps? Then, in 2002, another robot was sent up the shaft to drill a hole through the door and photograph what lay beyond. Sadly, the robot's view was blocked by a wall, so we will have to wait a little longer to uncover the shaft's secrets!

Fantasy or Fact?

At just 20 centimetres (8 inches) square, the two shafts rising from the King's chamber in the Great Pyramid at Giza are extremely narrow. For many years archaeologists thought they were just to let air into the chamber. But recent research shows that, when the pyramid was completed, the two shafts were in line with two stars – Sirius, and Thuban in the constellation of Draco. Many people now think the shafts were designed to guide the dead pharaoh's soul upwards to the Afterlife.

DID YOU KNOW? In 1837, a cartouche found in the Great Pyramid identified Khufu as its builder.

Pyramid designers and builders

The architects

The first pyramid was designed by Imhotep, for the pharaoh Djoser (reigned 2667–2648 BC). It was built at Saqqara, south of Giza, and when it was completed in about 2650 BC, it had a rectangular base and stepped sides. The true pyramid, with a square base and smooth-sloping sides, developed during the reign of Sneferu (reigned 2613–2589 BC). Sneferu was the father of Khufu, for whom the Great Pyramid at Giza was built.

WHO WAS Imhotep?

*Imhotep's tomb has not yet been discovered, and we don't know when he was born or died, but **inscriptions** have told us that he was the architect who designed the first pyramid, at Saqqara, around 4650 years ago. We also know that he was the pharaoh Djoser's **vizier**, or prime minister. The Egyptians respected Imhotep greatly, and in later centuries they began to worship him as a god of wisdom, writing and medicine.*

▽ *Archaeologists think that the pyramid builders probably made ramps, up which they could haul the blocks of stone.*

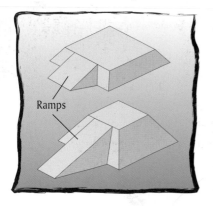

Ramps

Workers and construction methods

People once believed that the pyramids were built by slaves, but archaeologists now think that hundreds of skilled stonemasons were employed to cut the stone and the unskilled labour was carried out by thousands of peasant farmers. Each year the River Nile flooded, covering the fields for three or so months – farmers only had to work on the pyramids during this flood season.

No descriptions of pyramid-building have been found, so archaeologists do not know what methods were used. They are fairly certain that ramps were made so that the huge stone

Moving mountains

Another puzzle is how the Egyptians pulled the pyramid blocks up the construction ramp. The most likely answer is based on paintings like this. It shows a load of blocks being transported on a large wooden sledge, hauled by a team of men. Using a sledge would reduce the load to as little as one-tenth of its weight.

blocks could be hauled upwards. The ramps would have grown higher as the pyramid grew larger, but no one knows what shape they were. Some people think a single ramp was built at the front of the pyramid, while others believe the ramp spiralled up around it. Unless future **excavations** uncover new evidence, the pyramid-builders' techniques will remain a mystery.

River transport

Although we are not certain how pyramid blocks were moved on land, we do know they were floated on boats from the quarries to the pyramid site. The River Nile runs through the heart of Egypt, and boats were the main form of transport. Most were similar in shape to these model boats, which came from a tomb. Small boats were made from bundles of **papyrus** reeds. They were used for local travel and for fishing or hunting. Larger, wooden boats were used in war or to transport heavy loads long distances.

Just over 1000 years after they were first built, pyramids began to go out of fashion. They were meant to keep the **pharaohs** and their possessions safe for eternity, but no matter how many hidden entrances and false passages they contained, they were still looted by **tomb-robbers**. The pharaoh Thutmose I (reigned 1504–1492 BC) asked his architect Ineni to come up with a new, safer kind of tomb.

The Valley of the Kings

From then on, the **mummies** of Egypt's rulers were hidden away in rock tombs carved out of the sides of a remote valley in the desert mountains of Upper Egypt. Today the site is known as the Valley of the Kings. As far as safety went, however, the new rock-cut tombs were little improvement on the pyramids. When Egyptologists began excavating in the Valley in the 19th century, every tomb they came across was found to have been broken into in ancient times.

The forgotten tomb of Tutankhamen

Only one archaeological team was allowed to work in the Valley at a time, and in 1915 the permit passed to Howard Carter. By then, most archaeologists believed that no more tombs remained to be discovered, but Carter believed that at least one was still hidden.

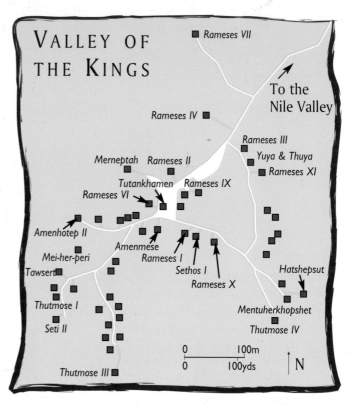

VALLEY OF THE KINGS

Rameses VII

To the Nile Valley

Rameses IV

Rameses III
Yuya & Thuya
Rameses XI

Merneptah Rameses II
Tutankhamen Rameses IX
Rameses VI

Amenhotep II

Amenmese
Mei-her-peri Rameses I

Tawsert
Sethos I
Rameses X
Hatshepsut

Thutmose I

Mentuherkhopshet
Seti II
Thutmose IV

0   100m
0   100yds   N

Thutmose III

△ *One of the world's most famous burial grounds, the Valley of the Kings is on the west bank of the River Nile, opposite the modern-day town of Luxor. More than 60 tombs have been found there, made up of corridors and chambers cut out of the limestone cliffs that surround the Valley.*

WHO WAS Howard Carter?

*Howard Carter (1874–1939) was just 17 when he arrived in Egypt. His first job was as an artist, copying tomb paintings. Later he trained as an excavator and in 1899 he was given a senior position in the Egyptian Antiquities Service. He resigned in 1903, and worked as an artist and dealer in **antiquities** until 1908, when financial support from Lord Carnarvon allowed him to return to **excavation**. Following his discovery of Tutankhamen's tomb in 1922, Carter spent the remaining 17 years of his life recording and analysing his finds.*

Little was known then about the pharaoh Tutankhamen (reigned 1336–1327 BC), but Carter hoped to change this. His search was funded by his sponsor, Lord Carnarvon (1866–1923), who was a wealthy amateur Egyptologist. The hunt took years, but on 4 November 1922 Carter's workers found a sunken staircase. At the bottom they uncovered the top part of a blocked doorway, which was coated in plaster and stamped with official **seals**. It seemed to be the entrance to a tomb. Carter dashed off a telegram to his sponsor, who was in England, and ordered his men to refill the staircase until Lord Carnarvon could join them.

▽ *This photograph shows the mysterious doorway found by Carter's team in November 1922. Further excavation uncovered 16 steps leading down to it.*

EYEWITNESS

'At last have made wonderful discovery in Valley; a magnificent tomb with seals intact; recovered same for your arrival; congratulations.'

(Howard Carter's 1922 telegram to Lord Carnarvon in England)

Tutankhamen's treasures

The tension mounts

Lord Carnarvon hurried to Egypt, and on 24 November 1922 excavation work began again. This time the whole doorway was uncovered, and stamped into the plaster at the bottom was a seal bearing one of Tutankhamen's royal titles. Carter and Carnarvon now knew they had found the pharaoh's tomb – but would they find anything left inside?

A long corridor full of rubble lay beyond the tomb entrance. As Carter's workers cleared it, they found evidence of a robbers' tunnel dug in ancient times. On 26 November, the excavators stood at the end of the emptied corridor, in front of a second doorway. Carter made a small hole in it and peered inside. To his amazement, the chamber beyond was crammed with goods – and everywhere was the glitter of gold!

△ This was the sight that met Carter's eyes when he peered into the first chamber of Tutankhamen's tomb. In the centre of the photograph is a couch with legs shaped like an animal's body.

The tomb had four chambers. Robbers had managed to break into one of them, but they had taken little. It seemed as though they had been caught and stopped. Hundreds of Tutankhamen's possessions remained inside. Even his mummy was still there, safe inside a stone **sarcophagus** and three richly decorated **coffins**.

WHO WAS Tutankhamen?

Tutankhamen's name is very well known today, but little is known about his life. No one is certain who his parents were. He became pharaoh in 1336 BC, on the death of the pharaoh Akhenaten. Therefore it is likely that Tutankhamen was Akhenaten's younger brother or son. Tutankhamen was only eight or nine when he was crowned. Less than ten years later, in 1327 BC, he died and was buried in the Valley of the Kings.

Fantasy or Fact?

A mystery surrounding Tutankhamen is how he died. Two major **post-mortems** were carried out on his mummified body. The first, in 1925, gave us his height (about 1.63 metres; 5 ft 4 in) and his age when he died (17 to 19 years old). By the time of the second post-mortem, in 1968, X-rays were available. They showed that Tutankhamen's skull had been damaged, suggesting that he was killed by an accidental or deliberate blow to the head. We may never know for certain, but some archaeologists now believe that Tutankhamen's short reign was brought to an end by murder!

▷ *Egyptian workers helped to excavate and clear Tutankhamen's tomb. The original position of each artefact was carefully recorded before it was removed for painstaking study, cleaning and preservation. Larger objects had to be taken apart and put back together once outside the tomb.*

Every object tells a story

It took Carter's team years to empty the tomb. Chairs and beds, chariots and weapons, musical instruments and games had been buried with the pharaoh, along with clothes, cosmetics and jewellery. There were also baskets of food, and a wreath of flowers which had been placed inside one of the coffins. Tutankhamen's tomb turned out to be the richest find in the history of **archaeology**, jam-packed with objects that give us a rare and vivid picture of upper-class life in ancient Egyptian times.

Royal regalia

The head of Tutankhamen's mummy was protected by this death mask made in solid gold. It portrays him in his everyday crown, called the nemes. In real life, no type of Egyptian crown seems to have been made of solid gold, and the nemes was actually made of striped cloth. Tutankhamen's mask shows another symbol of the pharaoh's power – the false beard, which in real life was made of wood and tied on with a strap.

Finding out about the pharaoh

Egyptian society

Written and visual evidence tells us that the ancient Egyptians worshipped their ruler, the pharaoh, as the living son of a god. They were so in awe of him that even nobles would kiss the ground below his feet. Everyone and everything in Egypt belonged to the pharaoh, and he was head of the government, the priesthood, the army and the law courts.

The **vizier**, or prime minister, led the government and, after the pharaoh, was the most important person in Egypt. Then came the high priests, who were responsible for all aspects of religion and worship, followed by the commanders-in-chief of the army and navy. Egypt was divided into 42 districts, called nomes, and each nome had its own governor, who reported to the vizier.

Below these top officials there were thousands of **scribes** who carried out day-to-day business, such as collecting taxes and maintaining law and order. The Egyptians did not use money, so taxes were paid in goods, such as grain and animals. Below the scribes were artists and other skilled craftworkers, and right at the bottom were all the hard-working farmers, who provided the food that kept everyone in Egypt alive.

Seat of power

Another of the treasures in Tutankhamen's tomb was a magnificent throne, made of wood coated in sheets of gold and silver. The back panel (left) shows Tutankhamen with his wife, Ankhesenamen. Gold was a holy material for the ancient Egyptians. They believed that the gods' bodies were made of gold, and they also associated gold with the Sun and everlasting life.

War and weapons

Only a few pharaohs actually took part in battles, but the pharaoh was always head of the army. Therefore pharaohs were often portrayed fighting, to symbolize their bravery – as in the painting on this box found in Tutankhamen's tomb. Egyptian armies were made up of foot soldiers, who fought with spears, swords and daggers, and charioteers armed with bows and arrows. In real life, a chariot would have held two men – a driver and an archer.

DID YOU KNOW? Even Queen Hatshepsut (reigned 1473–1458 BC) wore the pharaoh's beard!

TEMPLES AND GODS

The Egyptians worshipped hundreds of gods and goddesses. **Temples** were believed to be their earthly homes, and it was every **pharaoh**'s duty to build temples and to make sure that offerings were made to keep the gods happy. In return, the gods would bless the people with everything from good health and harvests to victory in battle. Like the pyramids, Egyptian temples were built from stone and have lasted through the ages. More have survived than any other kind of building.

The great temple complex at Karnak

Egypt's largest and most important holy site was at Karnak, near the modern-day town of Luxor. The temples and other buildings that can be seen there today were begun about 3500 years ago, but beneath the ground archaeologists have found traces of earlier structures dating back another 1500 years. Nearly every pharaoh added to Karnak, often tearing down earlier structures and reusing the stone to build new ones.

▽ *The tall stone pillars with the pyramid-shaped tops in this part of the Temple of Amun at Karnak are called obelisks. Egyptian rulers often had obelisks put up in front of temples, but many were removed from Egypt during the 19th century, including the 'Cleopatra's Needle' obelisks now in London and New York.*

◁ *A series of massive gateways lead into the Temple of Amun, each built by a different pharaoh. Beyond the first gateway is a courtyard, beyond the second is the* **hypostyle hall***, and deep in the heart of the temple is the shrine where, people believed, the god's spirit lived in his statue. These enormous carved and painted columns once held up the stone roof of the hypostyle hall.*

When European travellers arrived in Egypt in the 19th century, little was left of the temples' ancient glory. Great chunks of roof, walls and columns had collapsed, while the parts of the buildings that remained standing were largely buried in sand. Over the past hundred or so years, archaeologists have started on the vast task of **excavation** and **restoration**. The main temples have been excavated, but buried deep beneath them lies unexplored evidence which will keep archaeologists busy for many generations to come.

EYEWITNESS

'I seemed alone in the midst of all that is most sacred ...; a forest of enormous columns, adorned all around with beautiful figures, and various ornaments ...'

(Italian excavator Giovanni Belzoni, on entering the hypostyle hall in the Temple of Amun, 1816)

Archaeology Challenge

Sometimes **archaeology** is not only about excavating sites, but about rescuing them. In the 1960s, a dam was built across the River Nile, south of Aswan. The region's temples were in danger of vanishing under water, once the river rose behind the completed dam. An international appeal was launched for money to save the most important temples. It was possible then to take the temples apart and rebuild them on new sites. The largest building to be moved in this way was the great temple carved into the rock cliffs of Abu Simbel. It is fronted by 20-metre-high statues of its builder, the pharaoh Rameses II (reigned 1279–1213 BC).

Priests and worshippers

Archaeologists have built up a picture of how the Egyptians worshipped, both by studying **papyrus scrolls** containing hymns, prayers and official documents, such as records of temple offerings, and by looking at carvings and paintings on temple and **tomb** walls. Only the pharaoh and a few leading priests could approach the holiest part of the temple, called the **sanctuary**. Here was the **shrine**, where people believed the god's spirit lived in his statue. Ordinary people were sometimes allowed in the temple courtyard.

Galaxy of gods

The tall feather-plumed headdress tells us that the statue on the left is of Amun, the king of the Egyptian gods. Amun was usually portrayed in human form, although other gods were often shown as animals or with animal heads. Only the most important gods had their own temples and priests. Most of the major gods represented forces such as the Sun or the River Nile, or were linked with important events in life, such as birth or death.

▷ *Taweret, goddess of birth and protector of women and children, had a hippo's head and body. She was also shown with a lion's paws and a crocodile's tail.*

The gods' servants

The Egyptians called their priests 'servants of the gods'. They were mostly men, although until about 1600 BC it was common for noblewomen to serve as priestesses of the goddess of love, Hathor.

Priests did not hold public services and few worked at the temple all year round. Instead there was a rota system, with different groups spending one month at the temple doing their priestly duties, followed by three months at home doing their usual jobs. Most of a priest's duties were to do with the everyday organization of the temple complex – running libraries, workshops, storerooms and so on. Only a few special priests were allowed to serve the god by taking part in temple **rituals**.

Holy service

The most important temple rituals were all about caring for the statue in which the god's spirit was believed to live. Every day at dawn, a special priest would burn **incense**, to **purify** the air, and pour an offering of clean water in front of the god's shrine. The god's statue was then taken out, undressed and washed, before being clothed in clean linen and beautified with fresh make-up. Real food was served for the god's breakfast, and at similar rituals later in the day.

▷ *Thoth, god of wisdom and patron god of scribes, was shown as a baboon, an ibis bird or an ibis-headed man.*

Magic and medicine

In ancient Egypt, magic was central in everything from temple rituals to medical treatment. Magical charms called amulets were worn to bring people luck and protect them from harm. These came in many shapes, but the scarab beetle was one of the most popular. Although doctors were skilled at setting bones and making herbal remedies, people believed that the most effective cures were brought about by a combination of magic and medicine.

EVERYDAY LIFE OF THE WEALTHY

Pharaohs and their families were not the only Egyptians to be buried in rock-cut **tombs**. Nobles and wealthy government officials also commissioned craftsmen to create splendid tombs to house their mummified bodies throughout eternity. Tombs with wall-carvings or paintings are known as decorated tombs, and as many as 400 of them have been found in and around the Valley of the Kings.

*△ Nebamun is shown here hunting river birds. He has brought his wife (standing behind him) and daughter (sitting) along for the outing. He is standing on a small **papyrus**-reed boat and, in one hand, is holding a snake-shaped throwing stick, which was hurled at prey to stun or kill it.*

The tomb of Nebamun

Some of the finest wall-paintings are from the tomb of an official called Nebamun, who lived in the 1300s BC. The paintings show him and his family hunting, feasting and generally having a good time in the **Afterlife**. They can still be seen today, but not in Egypt. They are in the British Museum in London, which acquired them in 1821. The paintings are from a tomb at Thebes, discovered by the British consul Henry Salt, but the exact location of the tomb is now lost. The tomb was probably robbed by ancient Egyptian tomb-robbers soon after Nebamun was buried, and was empty when Henry Salt removed some of the wall-paintings.

Magical mirror of life

The Egyptians believed that the images in decorated tombs could magically supply the dead person's needs in the Afterlife. For instance, if a painting showed a noble hunting, then he would be able to enjoy this pastime in the Afterlife.

Archaeology Challenge

The decorated tombs in the Valley of the Kings are under threat, especially from the thousands of tourists who tramp through them every day. Moisture from their breath and body sweat harms the paintings, as do the electric lights that are needed to guide people through the darkness underground. Many of the finest tombs have now been closed, in order to protect them, but tourists will still be able to see their marvellous paintings. A project is underway to make replica tombs, using the latest laser-scanning and computer technology to create completely accurate 'virtual reality' copies.

The artists themselves are rarely shown, and there is little evidence of how they worked. Archaeologists believe that a sketch was made first, on a small board marked with a squared grid. A full-size grid was marked on to the tomb wall, and the sketch was scaled up and copied on to it. The final stage was to paint in all the glorious colour detail.

◁ Archaeologists think that using a grid helped artists to keep figures and objects in their paintings in proportion. For example, they could ensure that each lower arm was four squares of the grid long. People were nearly always shown with their eyes, chest and shoulders facing forwards.

Pastimes

The thrill of the chase

Like Nebamun, wealthy Egyptians enjoyed hunting and fishing, often going after much bigger prey than birds. Hippopotamuses and crocodiles lived in the River Nile in ancient times, while lions, ostriches and wild bulls roamed across the desert. Some tomb paintings show hunters dicing with death, trying to spear fierce river creatures. Others show them in their chariots chasing after wild desert animals.

Perfect party

Another of the beautiful paintings from Nebamun's tomb shows a banquet in full swing. Seated guests are waited on by servants. The women have longer hair than the men, and some men have shaved heads. Nearly everyone has a cone of perfumed ointment on their head. As the cones slowly melted, they kept people cool and smelling sweet.

Getting in the party spirit

When not out hunting, the wealthy loved to party. Guests at a banquet would wear their finest clothes and jewellery, and be served with beer, wine and a range of tasty dishes. Food left in tombs and shown in paintings tells us that the wealthy dined on a wide selection of farmed meats, including beef, lamb and goat, and wild game, such as antelope and gazelle. They also ate all sorts of vegetables and fruit, as well as bread and honey-sweetened cakes and pastries. Dishes were flavoured with herbs, such as mint and thyme, and spices, such as cumin and coriander.

Music to the ears

The paintings in Nebamun's tomb show that musicians and dancers provided entertainment for the guests at the banquet. Musicians often supplied a background beat by clapping their hands, as the three women to the left of the flute-player are doing in this wall-painting. Many musical instruments have been found in Egyptian tombs, including harps, lutes, flutes and tambourines, but we have no idea of what Egyptian music sounded like – they never wrote down the tunes.

▷ *This ancient Egyptian harp dates from between 1200 and 500 BC.*

Child's play

Children played with simple, home-made toys in ancient Egyptian times, including cloth or leather balls, and model animals carved from wood. Some of their games are still played by children today, including leapfrog and tug-of-war. Children from wealthy families had more playtime than the poor, of course, who had to work in the fields alongside their fathers or help their mothers at home.

Fantasy or Fact?

All this talk of tombs may give the impression that the Egyptians were miserable people who spent all their time thinking about death. Nothing could be further from the truth. Decorated tombs show us all the things the Egyptians enjoyed doing while they were alive, and that they loved life so much that they wanted to carry on experiencing the same pleasures throughout eternity!

Fashion

Cool clothing

Egypt is a hot country and the clothing was designed to keep people cool. Rich and poor people wore similar clothes, although the wealthy could afford better-quality fabric. The basic outfit for men was a kilt-like skirt, and for women, a long, sheath-like dress. The only underwear for both sexes was a **loincloth**, and most people wore sandals made from palm leaves or papyrus. By about the 1500s BC, wealthy men also sometimes wore a T-shaped tunic, while women wrapped a large pleated shawl around their body, tying it under their breasts. Young children went naked, and older ones dressed like their parents.

△ *This painting from the tomb of a wealthy court official, Sennedjem, at Deir el-Medina shows pleated clothing.*

Luxury linen

The clothes of most Egyptians, rich and poor, were made from linen, which was woven from the flax plant. Only the wealthy could afford the finest, whitest fabric, and by the 1300s BC, fashionable women were wearing linen so fine that it was see-through. Wall-paintings and carvings show that it became stylish to wear heavily pleated clothes, but archaeologists are not sure how the pleating was done. In one tomb they found this grooved wooden board, which may have been used to press pleats into clothing.

Finishing touches

Wealthy men and women also went in for elaborate hairstyles, make-up and jewellery. Hair was plaited or curled, and on special occasions people wore wigs. Children often had their heads shaved, apart from a single lock on one side of the head.

Archaeologists have a wide range of evidence for Egyptian clothes and beauty preparations, from **artefacts** placed in tombs to the images in wall-paintings and carvings. In 1974, they even found the remains of a wig-maker's workshop at Deir el-Bahri.

▷ *This gold and turquoise collar belonged to the daughter of pharaoh Amenemhat II (reigned 1922–1878 BC).*

Glittering prizes

Egyptians loved jewellery, and men and women wore necklaces, bracelets, armlets and anklets, as well as hair ornaments, rings and earrings. The most valuable pieces were made from gold or silver, and set with semi-precious stones, such as lapis lazuli, turquoise and carnelian. Most of the gold was mined in southern Egypt and Nubia, but silver was imported from a number of Mediterranean and western Asian countries. Valuable Egyptian goods, such as linen and **papyrus**, were exchanged in this kind of overseas trade.

Beautiful people

All sorts of cosmetics and beauty tools have been found in Egyptian tombs, from eye-paint and lip-paint to make-up bottles, mirrors, tweezers, razors, combs and hair-curling tongs. Both men and women wore make-up. Chemical tests have shown that green eye-paint was made from ground-up malachite (a copper ore) and black from galena (a lead ore). Red ochre (a type of earth) was used to make lip gloss and rouge for the cheeks.

EVERYDAY LIFE OF THE WORKERS

Archaeologists have excavated only a small number of sites that tell us about ancient Egyptian houses. This is partly because, unlike the grand stone pyramids and **temples**, Egyptian homes were mostly built from bricks made from sun-baked river mud – and mud-bricks crumble away far more quickly than stone. Another reason for the lack of evidence is that many modern-day villages have been built on and from the rubble of earlier ones – then, as now, most homes were built in the narrow strips of fertile land by the River Nile.

The workers' village of Deir el-Medina

Most of the ancient villages that have survived are close to the desert fringes. They were built for the craftsmen who worked on the decorated **tombs** and the pyramids. One of the best-preserved is the village of Deir el-Medina, which housed the families of the men building the rock-cut tombs in the Valley of the Kings. Although **artefacts** were found at the site in the early 19th century, the chief **excavation** work was carried out from 1905 to 1909 by Italian Ernesto Schiaparelli (1856–1928), and between 1917 and 1947 by Frenchman Bernard Bruyère (1879–1971). As well as the remains of the craftsmen's homes,

△ *At its largest, Deir el-Medina was made up of about 70 houses. The lower parts of the house walls were built from stone, cemented with mud and plaster, and this has helped them survive. The rest of the walls were made of mud bricks, which were plastered and whitewashed. The houses of the wealthy, in the towns and countryside, were built in a similar way, but were much larger, with many more rooms.*

a vast amount of written evidence was discovered, which gives a vivid picture of everyday work and home life.

Home sweet home

The excavations at Deir el-Medina revealed that the village had one central street, with houses on both sides separated by a few side alleys. The houses were narrow and all had roughly the same layout. Generally, each was made up of four small rooms, one behind the other. The front room, used by the women, seems to have been a reception area for visitors. Behind was a living room, used by the men, which was probably also used for sleeping. People may also have slept on the roof. The third room was used for storage, while the final room was where the women cooked the family meals.

▽ *This cross-section shows the plan of a typical house at Deir el-Medina, with four rooms and a staircase leading to the roof. Cellars beneath the house provided cool storage places for jars of food and drink.*

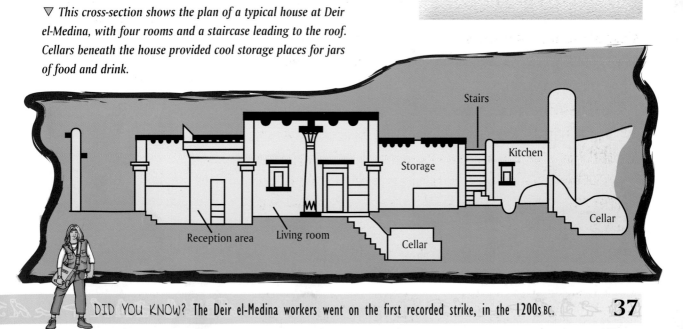

Stairs

Storage

Kitchen

Cellar

Reception area

Living room

Cellar

People at work

The village workers

The written evidence excavated at Deir el-Medina includes **papyri** and thousands of **ostraca** – the chips of stone or pottery which **scribes** used like notepads. As well as records of the workmen's tools, hours of work and wages, there are letters, poems and even laundry lists.

The craftsmen who worked on the tombs were stonemasons, carpenters, sculptors and painters, and their working 'week' was eight days long, followed by two days rest. Further down the social scale were the men who helped supply the craftsmen's everyday needs for food, water and so on. This included fishermen, gardeners, laundry-men, water-carriers and woodcutters.

Working families

Women were thought to be less important than men in ancient Egypt. They are rarely shown working as anything other than servants, as in this wooden model, or as musicians and dancers. Written evidence shows that some women also worked as bakers, weavers, gardeners and farmers. Most ordinary women spent their days cooking and cleaning. Girls helped their mothers, while boys worked alongside their fathers, learning their trade.

Tools of the trade

These wooden mallets and bronze chisels are stonemasons' tools found at Deir el-Medina. The chisels would have been used for shaping blocks of stone. Finer-pointed chisels, with wooden handles, would have been used for detailed work such as carving **hieroglyphs**.

The models of Meketra

In addition to the Deir el-Medina findings, archaeologists have collected a wealth of written and visual evidence from other sites throughout Egypt. The most vivid comes from beautifully detailed, painted wooden models, which were placed in tombs to provide servants for the **Afterlife**. One of the finest collections of these was found near Deir el-Bahri in 1920, in the tomb of Meketra, a powerful government official who died in about 2000 BC. The models, which formed a model estate, include a fascinating range of boats, as well as a brewery and bakery, a butcher's shop, a granary and carpenter's and weaver's workshops.

EYEWITNESS

'The beam [lit up] a little world of 4000 years ago, and I was gazing down into ... a myriad of brightly painted little men going this way and that ...'

(American archaeologist H. E. Winlock [1884–1950], on his first sight of the models of Meketra in 1920)

Carpenters at work

This exquisite 26-centimetre-high model of a carpenter's workshop is one of the treasures from Meketra's tomb. It shows the workshop bustling with activity, as men cut planks, drill and chisel holes, and plane down and smooth surfaces. Apart from palms, few trees grew in Egypt and the best-quality wood was imported from abroad. This made wooden objects, such as furniture, expensive, so the results of the carpenter's hard work were for his wealthy employer, not for his own home.

Farming and food

Farmers and landowners

As paid professionals, carpenters and other craftsmen were fairly well-off. The poorest Egyptians were the farmers. Most farming land in Egypt was owned by the **pharaoh**, his nobles or the temples. Farmers not only had to grow enough food to keep themselves and their families alive, but also had to pay a proportion of their grain harvest as a tax to the landowner. Tax-collecting scribes made regular visits to check that farmers got the best out of their land and did not cheat when declaring how much grain they had gathered at harvest time.

Important crops

The farmers' chief grain crops were wheat and barley. These were turned into bread and beer, which made up the main diet of ordinary Egyptians. Another important crop was flax, which was woven into cloth. All sorts of vegetables were grown too, from onions, garlic, beans and lentils, to cabbages, cucumbers, lettuces and peas. Fruit crops included dates, figs, grapes and melons. Although poor people rarely ate meat, farmers had eggs from their own ducks and chickens. They looked after their landowner's herds of cattle, and used oxen to do heavy work like pulling the plough.

Harvest time

This wall-painting of a harvest scene comes from the tomb of a wealthy scribe, called Menna, who died in about 1400 BC – and hoped to have lots of grain in the Afterlife! The farmer on the left is cutting grain with a wooden sickle, and the harvested corn is being carried away in a large basket.

Archaeology Challenge

Dental examination of mummified Egyptians' teeth shows that they were often ground down and worn away. Archaeologists discovered the cause of these bad teeth by analysing loaves of bread, which had been preserved for thousands of years in tombs. Bread was the main food of most Egyptians, rich and poor, but chewing on it must have given them terrible toothache. The ancient loaves of bread were full of stone grit, which came from the way grain was ground into flour by rubbing it between two stones.

Home brew

Beer was the favourite drink of ordinary Egyptians, but it was so thick and lumpy that it had to be sieved or sucked up through a wooden strainer, which was like a straw! Beer was made at home, by dissolving partly baked cakes of barley bread in water. This mixture was then sieved and left to ferment into alcohol. Dates, honey and spices were sometimes added to flavour the brew.

Water power

Crops will not grow without water, and because it hardly ever rains in Egypt, farmers rely on the River Nile. This lifting device is called a shaduf, and since ancient times people have used it to raise river water up on to farmland. Until it was dammed in the 1960s, the Nile flooded every year in June, covering the fields with rich mud and life-giving water. Farmers ploughed their fields and sowed their crops after the floods went down in October or November.

ARCHAEOLOGY TODAY

The story of **Egyptology** is by no means over. Each year, well over a hundred teams of Egyptian and foreign archaeologists are hard at work excavating and recording sites throughout Egypt. In other countries around the world, more teams of archaeologists are examining and conserving the **artefacts** held by their nations' museums. Some are continuing the long task of deciphering the **hieroglyphic** texts in Egypt and in the museum collections. The objects found in the past 200 or so years will keep people busy for hundreds of years to come!

Going over old ground

The modern-day emphasis on scientific **archaeology** means that **excavation** work is slower and more painstaking than it was in the early years of Egyptology. Much of it happens at sites that have already been excavated, where today's teams are searching for evidence that was missed the first time around.

△ *You can see clearly how erosion by the weather has damaged the Great **Sphinx** at Giza.*

A concern for modern Egyptologists is that many of the known sites are under threat. It is not just the **tombs** in the Valley of the Kings that are being harmed by exposure to tourists, but also monuments such as the Great Pyramid at Giza. Other ancient monuments are being damaged by weathering and by rising levels of underground water.

◁ *Dr Zahi Hawass examines a masked mummy, one of many found in 1996 at a cemetery discovered in the Bahariya Oasis, Egypt. It is estimated that the site could contain 10,000 mummies.*

EYEWITNESS

'I believe that we've only found about 30 per cent of Egyptian monuments; that 70 per cent of them still lie buried underneath the ground.'

(Dr Zahi Hawass, Undersecretary of State for the Giza Monuments, 1997)

Nosing out the new

The picture is not all doom and gloom, though, and exciting new discoveries continue to be made – even at well-known sites. In 1990, the leading Egyptian archaeologist Dr Zahi Hawass (born 1947) made an extraordinary find at Giza, close to the Great Pyramid. He discovered a cemetery which turned out to contain more than 40 tombs belonging to the workers who built the pyramids over 4500 years ago. By studying the workers' bones, Hawass's team learned that the pyramid builders died relatively young – between the ages of 30 and 35. By contrast, officials lived almost twice as long.

In 2002, a Swiss team literally stumbled across a previously unknown pyramid buried in the sand just a few kilometres to the south of Giza. It is not a large pyramid, and there was no **mummy** inside, but it is thought to have belonged to a **pharaoh**'s wife, daughter or sister. The story of Egyptology is still unfolding, and who knows what amazing finds may lie just around the corner!

TIMELINE OF ANCIENT EGYPT

There were three great ages in ancient Egyptian history, known as the Old, Middle and New Kingdoms. Each age was followed by a period of unrest, civil war and invasion. These periods are known as the Intermediate Periods.

The events in ancient Egyptian history took place so long ago that historians cannot be certain of the exact dates. You may discover that the dates given in this book are slightly different to those found in other sources.

About 5000 BC
The narrow strip of fertile land by the River Nile becomes known as Lower Egypt (the northern region) and Upper Egypt (the southern region).

About 3500 BC
Hieroglyphic writing develops.

About 3100 BC
Lower and Upper Egypt are united under one ruler, called Menes.

2686–2181 BC
OLD KINGDOM

2650 BC
Egypt's first pyramid is built at Saqqara, for Pharaoh Djoser.

About 2580 BC
The Great Pyramid at Giza is completed, for Pharaoh Khufu.

2181–2055 BC
First Intermediate Period
Civil war divides and weakens Egypt.

2055–1650 BC
MIDDLE KINGDOM

2055 BC
Upper and Lower Egypt are reunited by Mentuhotep II. He moves the capital from Memphis (in the north) to Thebes (in the south). He and his successors restore Egypt's wealth and power, and architecture, literature and other arts flourish. The first great temples are built at Karnak.

1650–1550 BC
Second Intermediate Period
The Hyksos invade from Palestine and nearby, and conquer Lower Egypt.

1550–1069 BC
NEW KINGDOM

1550 BC
The Hyksos are driven out of Egypt and Ahmose I is crowned pharaoh. During the New Kingdom, Egypt becomes the strongest, wealthiest nation in the Middle East.

1504–1492 BC
Pharaoh Thutmose I reigns. He is the first Egyptian ruler to have a rock-cut tomb in the Valley of the Kings.

1352–1336 BC
Pharaoh Akhenaten rules Egypt. He forces his people to worship a single sun god, Aten.

1336–1327 BC
Tutankhamen is pharaoh. Egyptians may once again worship many gods.

1279–1213 BC
Rameses II (Rameses the Great) rules Egypt. The temple at Abu Simbel, beautiful additions to the temple complex at Karnak and many other monuments are built during his reign.

1184–1153 BC
Rameses III reigns. Egypt is invaded by foreign armies from the north and its power begins to decline.

1069–747 BC
Third Intermediate Period
Civil war divides Egypt once more.

747–332 BC
LATE PERIOD

525–404 BC
Persia invades and takes control of Egypt. After the Persians are defeated, the country returns to Egyptian rule.

About 450 BC
The Greek traveller and historian Herodotus visits Egypt.

343–332 BC
Persia invades again, and regains control of Egypt.

332 BC–AD 395
GREEK-ROMAN PERIOD

332 BC
The Persians are overthrown by the armies of Alexander the Great. Egypt becomes part of his Greek Empire.

305–30 BC
After Alexander's death, the throne passes to one of his generals, Ptolemy. Ptolemy and his heirs rule Egypt.

196 BC
The Rosetta Stone is carved.

51–30 BC
Ptolemy's last heir, Cleopatra VII, rules. She kills herself when Egypt is conquered by the Romans and becomes part of the Roman Empire.

TIMELINE OF EGYPTOLOGY

1798–1801
The foundations of Egyptology are laid during the invasion of Egypt by the French emperor Napoleon. His army is accompanied by a team of artists and scientists, who carry out the first detailed study of ancient Egyptian monuments. In 1799, one of Napoleon's soldiers finds the Rosetta Stone – this will be the key to understanding the hieroglyphic writing of the ancient Egyptians.

About 1800–50
Foreign collectors flock to Egypt in search of antiquities. Many are adventurers who loot sites, causing the loss or damage of countless ancient artefacts. Others are scholars, such as the German Egyptologist Karl Lepsius, who build on the work of the French expedition.

1822
French scholar Jean-François Champollion cracks the code of the Rosetta Stone and becomes the first person since ancient times to be able to read hieroglyphs.

1858
The plundering of ancient sites ends when the French Egyptologist Auguste Mariette is put in charge of excavation in Egypt. Mariette founds the Egyptian Antiquities Service (now the Supreme Council for Antiquities) and the Egyptian Museum, in Cairo.

1881
Frenchman Gaston Maspero succeeds Mariette as head of the Antiquities Service and the Egyptian Museum. A tomb containing mummies of over 50 pharaohs, queens, other royals and courtiers is excavated at Deir el-Bahri, near the Valley of the Kings.

1880s
The scientific recording, excavation and preservation of archaeological sites is pioneered by the great British archaeologist Flinders Petrie.

1898
Serious excavation work begins in the Valley of the Kings. Many royal tombs are discovered, including that of one of Egypt's most powerful pharaohs, Thutmose III (reigned 1479–1425 BC).

1899
American archaeologist George Reisner begins excavations in Egypt, at Koptos near Luxor, setting similarly high standards to those of Petrie.

1903–05
At the temple complex of Karnak, near Luxor, French Egyptologist Georges Legrain unearths the largest find of royal statues ever made in Egypt.

1905–09
Italian Egyptologist Ernesto Schiaparelli excavates the village of Deir el-Medina, uncovering the homes and tombs of workmen who built the royal tombs in the Valley of the Kings.

1920
At Deir el-Bahri, the tomb of the government official Meketra (died about 2000 BC) is excavated by American archaeologist Herbert Winlock. The discoveries include a splendid collection of wooden models which illustrate many aspects of ancient Egyptian life.

1922
In the Valley of the Kings, British Egyptologist Howard Carter discovers the magnificent tomb of Pharaoh Tutankhamen (reigned 1336–1327 BC).

1954
At Giza, the Egyptian archaeologist Kamal el-Mallakh makes an astounding discovery at the foot of the Great Pyramid of Pharaoh Khufu (reigned 2589–2566 BC) – a pit containing the pieces of the pharaoh's boat. When put back together, it is over 43 metres long – the largest ancient Egyptian boat that has ever been discovered.

1960s
An international rescue effort saves more than 20 temples and other ancient holy sites from being flooded by the construction of a new dam to the south of Aswan, in Upper Egypt. The monuments are taken apart and rebuilt on higher ground.

1990
Egyptian archaeologist Dr Zahi Hawass discovers the cemetery where the workers who built the Giza pyramids were buried.

1993
Archaeologists use a tiny robot camera to explore one of the shafts in the Great Pyramid at Giza.

1996
At the Bahariya Oasis in Egypt's Western Desert, a huge cemetery dating from the Greek-Roman period (332 BC–AD 395) is discovered. It is believed to contain as many as 10,000 mummies.

2002
A few kilometres to the south of Giza, Swiss archaeologists find the ruins of a pyramid which was built more than 4500 years ago. Around 110 pyramids have now been discovered in Egypt.

Afterlife

The ancient Egyptians believed that a person's spirit, memory and personality did not end with their death, but carried on to enjoy life in another world – the Afterlife.

antiquities

Objects or buildings that have survived since ancient times.

archaeology

The scientific excavation and study of the remains of past societies, such as buildings, artwork, dead bodies, and tools, pottery and other objects.

artefact

An object made by people, such as a tool or an ornament. Archaeologists often use the word 'artefacts' to describe the objects they find that were made by people in past times.

astronomy

The scientific study of the stars, planets and other space bodies that make up the universe.

burial goods

Objects buried with a dead body.

canopic jars

Four special jars used to store the intestines, liver, lungs and stomach of a mummified body.

cartouche

In Egyptian archaeology, a cartouche is an oval frame around the names of a god, a pharaoh or a member of the pharaoh's family.

civil war

A war between people who belong to the same country or nation.

coffin

The box in which a dead person's body is buried.

Coptic

The language of the Copts, a people descended from the ancient Egyptians.

courtier

A person who attends a royal court.

demotic

A simplified form of ancient Egyptian hieroglyphs.

dig (see **excavation**)

Egyptology

The study of the language, customs, ideas, art and history of ancient Egypt.

engineering

The use of scientific knowledge to design structures and machines, as well as tools, materials and other products.

excavation

The careful process used by archaeologists to dig up ground when looking for buried artefacts.

export

To send or take goods to another country.

famine

A long-lasting shortage of food that causes widespread hunger and death.

hieratic

A flowing form of writing based on hieroglyphs.

hieroglyphs

The earliest form of Egyptian writing, in which pictures stand for sounds or words.

hypostyle hall

A temple hall with a roof held up by many columns.

incense

A substance that gives off a pleasing scent when burned.

inscription

In archaeology, a historical or religious record that is carved, painted or written on a hard surface such as stone or metal.

loincloth

A piece of cloth worn around the hips.

medieval

Relating to the Middle Ages, the period in European history between ancient and modern times (about AD 500 to 1500).

mummy

A dead body that has been specially preserved to stop it rotting away. The process of doing this is called mummification.

ostraca (singular ostracon)

A flake of stone or piece of broken pottery used in ancient times for making rough notes and sketches.

papyrus (plural papyri)

A tall river plant, and the name of a kind of paper made from its reed-like stems. The ancient Egyptians used the reeds to make everything from paper, baskets and rope, to sandals, mats and small boats.

pharaoh

The title given by the ancient Egyptians to their kings. The word comes from the ancient Egyptian name for a royal palace – the 'per-aa', or Great House.

pilgrim

A person who makes a special journey to a holy site.

post-mortem

When doctors examine a dead body to find out how the person died.

prehistoric

The time before writing was invented and history was recorded.

preservation

Saving something from being lost, damaged, or slowly crumbling or rotting away.

purify

To cleanse and make pure.

radiocarbon dating

A way of working out how long ago an animal or plant died. All living things contain tiny amounts of a substance called carbon-14. After something dies, the amount of carbon-14 slowly diminishes. Because scientists know how long this takes, they can work out how long ago an animal or plant died by the amount of carbon-14 left in it.

restoration

When a building, painting or other object is repaired or cleaned, to return it to its former glory.

ritual

The special words and actions of a religious service or ceremony.

sanctuary

A holy place, such as a church or temple, as well as the holiest place inside it, such as the altar.

sarcophagus

A coffin carved from stone.

scribe

Someone who could write – one of the officials and priests who carried out the everyday business of running ancient Egypt.

scroll

A roll of paper. In ancient Egypt, scrolls were made by joining several sheets of papyrus paper together.

seal

A piece of clay stamped with signs, pictures and writing. Seals were used to mark ownership, so, for example, seals stamped with a pharaoh's name showed that a tomb belonged to him.

shrine

A sacred place, usually where people worship the body or statue of a god, saint or other holy person.

sphinx

In ancient legends, the sphinx was a monster with the body of a lion and the head of another creature, usually human. The ancient Egyptians carved many sphinx statues, large and small, but the most famous is the 20-metre (66-foot)-high Great Sphinx that sits in front of the pyramids of Giza.

survey

A detailed examination or investigation of a building or place, which often includes taking measurements so that an accurate record or map can be drawn up.

temple

A building in which people worship, especially in ancient or non-Christian religions.

tomb

A special chamber or room, or a hole specially cut into the ground where a dead person's body is buried.

vizier

The person who ran a pharaoh's government, rather like a modern-day prime minister.

FURTHER READING

Ancient Egypt

The British Museum Illustrated Encyclopedia of Ancient Egypt, Geraldine Harris & Delia Pemberton (British Museum Press, 1999)

The Egyptian News, Scott Steedman (Walker Books, 1997)

The Life and World of Cleopatra, Struan Reid (Heinemann Library, 2002)

The Life and World of Tutankhamen, Brian Williams (Heinemann Library, 2002)

Tutankhamun: the life and death of a Pharaoh, David Murdoch (Dorling Kindersley, 1998)

Archaeology

Archaeology: Discovering the Past, John Orna-Ornstein (British Museum Press, 2002)

The Mystery of the Hieroglyphs, Carol Donoughue (British Museum Press, 1999)

Abu Simbel 27
Afterlife 12, 15, 16, 17, 30, 31, 39, 40
animals 4, 15, 24, 32, 33, 35
antiquities 6, 21
architecture 4, 18
army 10, 24, 25
art 4, 10, 31
artists 24
astronomy 4, 11
Aswan Dam 27

beer 32, 40, 41
Belzoni, Giovanni 6, 27
boats 4, 10, 19, 30, 39
bread 41
bricks 36
Brugsch, Emile 13
Bruyère, Bernard 36
burial goods 12, 13

canopic jars 14
Carnarvon, Lord 21, 22
carpenters 39, 40
Carter, Howard 20, 21, 22, 23
cartouche 9, 17
CAT scanner 15
Champollion, Jean-François 9
chariots 23, 25, 32
children 10, 28, 33, 34, 35
clothes 23, 32, 34, 35, 39
coffins 12, 13, 15, 22, 23
cosmetics 23, 35
craft-workers 24, 36, 38, 40
crops 40, 41
crown 24

Deir el-Bahri 12–13, 35, 39
Deir el-Medina 36–38

education 10, 11
Egyptian Antiquities Service 6, 13, 21
Egyptology 5, 13, 42
engineering 4, 16
epigraphy 8

farmers 18, 24, 38, 40, 41
food 23, 24, 29, 32, 37, 38, 40

games 23, 33
Giza 5, 16, 18, 42, 43
gods 14, 15, 18, 24, 25, 26–29
gold 23, 24, 25, 35
government 10, 20–25, 30

hairstyles 32, 35
Hawass, Dr Zahi 43
Herodotus 14, 37
hieroglyphs 8, 9, 11, 38
houses 4, 36, 37
hunting 19, 30, 31, 32

Imhotep 18
Ineni 20

jewellery 6, 23, 32, 35

Karnak 26–27

language 5, 8–11

magic 29
Mariette, Auguste 6
medicine 4, 18, 29
Meketra 39
money 24, 37
mummies 12–15, 16, 20, 22, 24, 41, 43
museums 6, 9, 30, 42
musical instruments 23, 33

Napoleon 5, 6, 9, 17
navy 24
Nebamun 30–33
Nile, River 4, 11, 13, 18, 19, 20, 27, 28, 32, 36, 39, 41

obelisks 26
ostraca 11, 38

paintings 4, 28, 30, 31, 32, 34
papyrus 8, 10, 11, 12, 19, 27, 28, 34, 35, 38
Petrie, Sir William Flinders 7
pharaohs 4, 12, 13, 16, 17, 18, 20–25, 26, 27, 30, 40, 43

priestess 15
priests 10, 14, 24, 28, 29
pyramids 4, 5, 16–19, 20, 26, 36, 42, 43

radar 13
radiocarbon dating 7
Reisner, George 7
restoration 27
robot camera 17
Rosetta Stone 9
rulers 9, 12, 13, 20, 24

Saqqara 18
sarcophagus 15, 17, 22
scarab 29
Schiaparelli, Ernesto 36
scribes 10, 11, 24, 38, 40
scroll 10, 11, 28
sequence dating 7
servants 32, 38, 39
shaduf 41
silver 35
slaves 18, 37
Sphinx 5
stonemasons 18

taxes 10, 24, 40
temples 4, 5, 26–29, 36, 40
tomb-robbers 12, 13, 16, 20, 22
tombs 12, 13, 16, 19, 20, 28, 30, 31, 32, 33, 34, 35, 36, 38, 39, 40
tourists 5, 31, 42
toys 33
trade 35
Tutankhamen 21–25

Valley of the Kings 12, 20, 23, 30, 31, 36, 42
villages 36
vizier 18, 24

war 19, 25
weapons 23, 25
women 28, 29, 32, 33, 34, 35, 37, 38
wood 39
writing 8, 11